High School
Grand Slam

Perfect Misfits LLC
An Independent Publishing Company

HIGH SCHOOL GRAND SLAM

An Educational GPS
Student Edition

Joyce A. Sessoms, M.Ed

"Exceptional! A blast of fresh air for parents of high school bound students! Meticulously plotted and arranged for any transitioning eighth grader as well as current students who are trying to successfully complete their high school journey. [This book] offers parents and students a view of the big picture— with pages for reflective thinking, thus minimizing the risks of poor planning."

Linda J. Schenck
Laurel School District Asst. Superintendent, Retired

Dedicated

To My Children
Gary Flowers and Cheryl Flowers
I thank God for molding you and shaping you into the amazing
adults that you have become. I am privileged to be chosen to be
your mother! You bring much joy to my life.
We share a forever love.

To Our Youth
Recognize the greatness within you that is waiting, tapped into
and released for the betterment of the world.

To Their Parents
To you who chose the path of resistance and accepted the
responsibility to train your children with strength and wisdom
in the parenting role when it would have been so much easier
to just be a friend.

"We have a powerful
potential in our youth,
and we must have the
courage to change
old ideas and practices
so that we may direct
their power toward
good ends."

–Mary McLeod Bethune,
Educator Founder of Bethune-Cookman College, 1875-1955

CONTENTS

INTERACTIVE ACADEMIC & CAREER PLANNING

You are about to turn a page in your life.

Can You Believe It?

YOU MADE IT TO HIGH SCHOOL!
CONGRATULATIONS!

High School Name: _____

Mascot: _____

Counselor: _____

Principal: _____

School Colors: _____

Graduation Year:_____

Students...
Get ready for one of the most exciting
journeys of your life!

Information is POWER!

Seek it.

Absorb it.

Use it!

Introduction

High School Grand Slam, Student Edition, is a unique tool that has been carefully designed and structured to assist you in selecting and navigating your path through high school. However, it is important to note that *High School Grand Slam* is not the only source of information you will need for your high school journey. It merely provides a foundation for you to understand what is expected of you and what you should expect from your high school experience.

High School Grand Slam explains key terms and guides you through high school step-by-step. We have even included useful tips to help you decide what the best fit for you will be after graduation. These tips cover options such as college, military service, taking over the family business, working for someone else, or starting your own enterprise.

We believe asking questions and being curious are essential to discovering the truth. It is important to seek knowledge and understanding and this personal interactive journal is a great tool to help you achieve this.

Keep your journal nearby, review it often, and create a plan to achieve both your short-term and long-term goals. By doing so, you'll be able to make informed decisions about your future, instead of simply hoping that you are on the right path towards graduation and your desired career.

High School Overview

Very Important Things You Need to Know!

To set yourself up for success, it's crucial to decide that you want to be an outstanding high school student, not a mediocre one. This doesn't necessarily mean that you need to be a straight-A student, but you can strive to perform at your highest potential in all aspects of your life. This decision is significant because it will determine your level of growth and maturity throughout the next four years.

The easy question/answer format of this interactive journal will help guide you through the learning process involved with high school and provide you with information you can use to be the most successful in attaining your goals.

What is required of me in high school?

High school is a different experience in many ways. You will come across new terms that might be unfamiliar to you, such as "credits" and "grade point average." You will be given an explanation for these terms later in the book. However, you must be accountable for your learning by attending school every day, being punctual, participating in class, taking effective notes, managing your time, and studying independently. Remember, the key is to put your best effort in high school.

Thoughts & Notes:

Because you have made it this far in your academic career, you should have the utmost confidence that **you have what it takes to succeed.**

READING is, and will always be, one of the major keys to progressing forward in any venue.

How do I know which school is my best fit?

Community College is a two (2) year college that offers an associate degree College/University is an institution of higher learning that takes approximately four (4) years to complete and offers bachelor's degrees. A college or university may also offer master's (which may be earned after completion of the bachelor's degree) and doctoral degrees (which may be earned after completion of the master's degree). The number of years it takes to complete these programs is contingent upon any factors.

Trade/Technical School is a school that teaches skilled trades such as carpentry, electronics, automotive, cosmetology, web design, etc.

To find the "best fit" for your interests and abilities, make sure you read the mission statement of the college prior to applying. You'll want to look at more than the degree programs they offer to be sure extra-curricular activities, location, cost, size of the campus, student body, and other aspects fit your preferences.

What if I decide that college isn't for me?

It is crucial to put in your utmost effort during high school. The reality is that regardless of whether you decide to attend college or not, you will eventually have to provide for yourself as an adult. You have to take responsibility for your future and not rely on anyone else.

Therefore, consider pursuing a military career, taking business courses to become a small-business owner (entrepreneur), or getting valuable training and experience to become a competitive employee. In case you must ask, *dropping out of high school is* not an option.

Important points to focus on:

- Start making life plans early.
- Follow through on your plans.
- Adjust your plans/goals as needed.
- Let nothing stand in the way of achieving your goals.
- Stay focused.

Search through magazines and newspapers for pictures of the kind of house you want to live in, the style of clothes you want to wear, the model of the car you want to drive, the type of career you desire, etc. Then, cut these photos out and tape them on a board to hang in your bedroom or wherever you spend most of your time. This constant reminder of your future goals will help keep you on track. Be sure to thoroughly research your career choice to make sure that the salary and job responsibilities will help you afford the type of lifestyle you want.

What can I expect from my guidance counselor?

In high school, you've been assigned a guidance counselor. There are hundreds of students, and only two or three faculty members are assigned this responsibility, so seniors get priority.

But, if a freshman, sophomore, or junior takes the *initiative*, guidance counselors are eager to work with you in mapping out your career options early on. You can make an appointment to speak with your counselor or get a pass from your teacher to visit the guidance office.

Along with principals, teachers, and staff, your guidance counselor is willing to work closely with you and your parents to offer the help needed to attain your educational goals. They are also available to address any interests or academic, social, or emotional concerns you may have. In the guidance office, information is available to help you with study habits, class scheduling, career pathways, college and career planning, personal counseling, conflict resolution, and more.

We encourage you to spend time in your guidance office resource room and ask lots of questions about scholarships, colleges, and careers. You will need the help of your parents, counselors, and teachers throughout this process.

Important Stuff Here ✓

How can I become involved in school life?

Get involved!

Your high school experience will only be as good as you make it. Don't be afraid to try new things and meet new people. This is all a part of the learning and growing process you will experience during your high school years. You can also develop good leadership and communication skills when you become part of a team. See what your school has to offer by way of sports activities, clubs, and organizations that you can join if you meet eligibility requirements.

Here are some exciting activities that may be available at your school:

- Baseball / Basketball / Wrestling / Cheerleading
- Golf / Track / Soccer / Softball
- Basics / Band / French Club / Spanish Club
- Yearbook / Chorus / Field Hockey / Key Club
- Student Government Association
- Business Professional Association

Remember, **volunteering** for a worthy cause or organization is very important. Volunteering to help others helps to build character and integrity.

Colleges and employers like to see this on your resumé! In some states, you can even earn a credit if you volunteer **90** documented/verified/ approved hours a year. Please see your guidance counselor for more information.

A lot of the students at my school are older than I am. Is there going to be a problem with violence, drugs, gangs, and bullying?

Great question. No particular high school in rural or suburban America is that much different from any other high school when it comes to these issues. Schools located in metropolitan areas may experience these problems to a greater degree due to the large and diversified number of students. But, people are going to be people.

Your school administrators strive toward *prevention* rather than *reaction*. Don't allow yourself to become part of the problem, but rather the solution. Maintain your integrity in tough situations. If you have concerns, feel free to address these issues with your principals, parents, counselors, resource officers, teachers, or staff. A Wellness Center or similar facility may also be available in your school for your use.

I was diagnosed with a learning disability and, in my previous school, I received extra help in the classroom to learn and keep up with the other students. Will I get that same help in high school?

Yes. Your parents and teachers had concerns about your academic, emotional, or social growth, so they sought the help of a professional. Sometimes a disability can make you feel like you're all alone, but you're not. Once the areas you need help with are identified, a team is assigned to develop what is called your IEP (Individualized Educational Plan).

The IEP lists detailed instructions regarding how you learn and retain information best, as well as other helpful information. The team, which includes you, your parents, teachers, and professionals, will meet at least once a year to evaluate the effectiveness of the plan that was developed. Your IEP information is kept confidential, and it will follow you throughout your educational career.

Virtual Learning

It is learning so...IT COUNTS!

While there are pros and cons to virtual learning, let's take a moment to explore the general how to's for success:

- Create quiet, comfortable surroundings
- Put distractions away
- Be prepared
- Be on time
- Dress appropriately
- Turn camera on
- Mute the mic
- Do not eat or drink during a class
- Pay attention
- Be respectful
- Take notes
- Do not play with the computer or other devices
- Have FUN!

Important Stuff Here ✔️

A.I.

Do not let your computer think for you.

Today are many programs that use A.I. and when this book is published, no doubt there will be many more!

A.I. stands for: Artificial Intelligence. It can be a good tool; however, you have natural intelligence and *learning* will increase your knowledge and brain power.

It is exciting to use your brain to be creative, to grow emotionally, to reason and explain your work, and to be able to think and recall information.

Be aware: there are programs that check your work to see if you used A.I. Make sure the writing, math, science, etc. and homework *you do* comes from *you!*

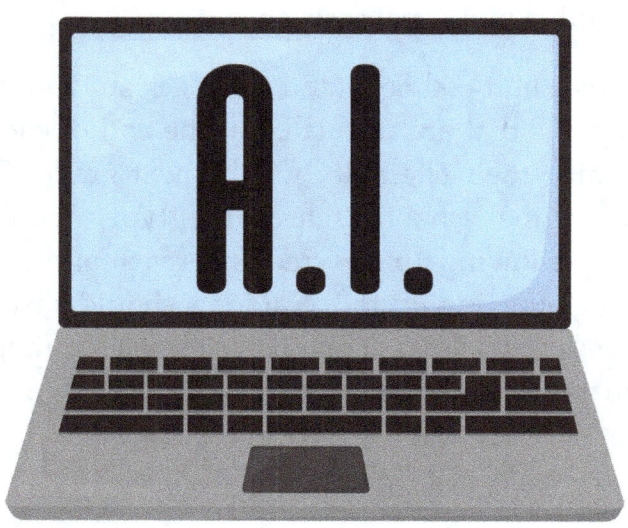

Important Stuff Here ✔

Important Terms You Really Need to Know

Student Success Plan (SSP)– Encompasses a *minimum of five years* (four years of high school and one year beyond high school), developed and updated at least annually by the student, the student's adviser, at least one other staff member, and the student's parent(s), guardian(s), or relative caregiver. The student's plan includes courses needed to prepare for immediate entry into the workforce or opportunities in post-secondary education. The plan also includes the support services necessary for the student to graduate from high school. An additional year of high school may be an option for inclusion in the Student Success Plan.

Support Services – Available in the form of educational interventions such as tutoring; extra time before school, in school, or after school; summer school; an extra year(s) of high school; or any other strategy that provides the student with educational assistance.

Credits–High school (and college students) earn course credits that are calculated at the end of each year to determine their eligibility for the next grade. Credits depend on the school's scheduling type, with block scheduling allowing up to 8 credits per year and semester scheduling allowing up to 7. Students should check with their counselor or registrar about promotion requirements, which may vary by state.

Thoughts & Notes:

Grade 9

At the end of your **freshman year (grade 9),** if you have earned **5 credits (1 of which must be English, and 1 of which must be math**), you will become a sophomore. Your school may have other exceptions to this rule. Some schools offer students the PSAT (Pre-Standardized Achievement Test), which can be used as an indicator of how well you will score on the actual SAT.

Grade 10

At the end of your **sophomore** year (**grade 10**), you need to have earned a total of **10 credits (2 of which must be English, and 2 of which need to be math** – your credits are added together each year) to pass to the next grade. In some states, this is the year you can take driver's education as a credited course for no charge.

Grade 11

In your third year of high school (**grade 11**), you are considered a **junior** if you have met the requirements. This means that you have already earned **10 credits** and are attempting to earn at least **16 credits** by the end of the school year (**3 of which must be English, and 3 of which must be math**). You should also be focusing on taking your college entrance exam, the SAT (Standardized Achievement Test).

Grade 12

Senior year (grade 12) This is the final year of high school, so **keep working hard**. *This is not the time to slack off* — quite the contrary. Colleges are looking for rigorous coursework during your senior year. To be considered for graduation, you must have earned **24 credits** or the number of credits for your state as determined by the governing Department of Education and school district guidelines.

Important Stuff Here ✅

Sample Graduation Requirements

Classes Required	Credits Needed
English	4
Math	4
Social Studies	3
Science	3
Physical Education	1
Health	0.5
Career Pathway	3
Electives	5.5
TOTAL	24

Sample Grading Chart

Letter	Percentage	Value
A	93-100	Exceptional Performance
B	85-92	Superior Performance
C	75-84	Average Performance
D	67-74	Poor Performance
F	> 66	Failing

It is your responsibility to find out what the graduation requirements are for your school, since they vary from state to state and district to district.

Sample Student Credit Map

Student Name: Molly Pace   ID# 6035287

Grade: 10   Career Pathway: Foreign Language

Counselor: Mr. Adams   Date Completed: MM-DD-YYYY

Courses Required for Graduation	Credits Needed	9th Grade Freshman Year	10th Grade Sophomore Year	11th Grade Junior Year	12th Grade Senior Year
ENGLISH	4	English 9 or Pre-AP English B-1 Credit	English 10 or AP/Honors Eng. A-1 Credit	English 11 or AP/Honors Eng. A-1 Credit	English 12 or AP/Honors Eng. A-1 Credit
MATH	4	Algebra 1 or AP/Honors Geometry B-1 Credit	Geometry or AP/Honors Alg. 2 B-1 Credit	Algebra 2 or AP Trigonometry B-1 Credit	Trigonometry or AP Calculus A-1 Credit
SOCIAL STUDIES	3	U.S. History or AP/Honors U.S. History B-1 Credit	World History or AP/Honors World History B-1 Credit	Civics/Economics or AP/Honors Civics/Econ. A-1 Credit	
SCIENCE	3	Physical Science or AP/Honors Science A-1 Credit	Biology or AP/Honors Biology A-1 Credit	Chemistry or AP/Honors Chemistry A-1 Credit	Anatomy & Physiology A-1 Credit
PHYSICAL EDUCATION	1	Physical Education A-1 Credit			Weights B-1 Credit
HEALTH	0.5		Health A-0.5 Credit		
CAREER PATHWAY	3	Spanish 1 A-1 Credit	Spanish 2 A-1 Credit	Spanish 3 A-1 Credit	Spanish 4 A-1 Credit
ELECTIVE CREDITS	5.5	Theater B-1 Credit	Driver's Ed. B-0.25 Credit Cultural Studies 1 A-1 Credit	Cultural Studies 2 B-1 Credit Psychology A-1 Credit	Cultural Studies 3 B-1 Credit AP Psychology A-1 Credit
TOTAL CREDITS EARNED	24	7 Credits	7 Credits Combine Grades 9+10 = 14 Credits	7 Credits Combine Grades 9+10+11 = 21 Credits	7 Credits Combine Grades 9+10+11+12 = 28 Credits
MINIMUM CREDITS REQUIRED TO ADVANCE TO THE NEXT GRADE		5 Credits	10 Credits	16 Credits	24 Credits

Credit blocks contain course name, final grade and number of credits earned. Blocks containing two courses include regular education courses at the top and AP or Honors courses underneath. Even if you have earned enough credits in other subject areas, many school districts require students to pass both English and Math each year to be eligible to advance to the next grade. Graduation requirements and course selections vary from state to state and district to district.

Career Pathway

This is a combination of three (3) different courses that are offered in the same discipline (e.g. performing arts, agriscience, business, foreign language) that a student takes over the course of their high school career. It is suggested that students select a career pathway—a specific area of interest that can lead to an area of study in college and eventually a career by grade 10 so that they can complete the requirements before graduation.

GPA – Grade Point Average

This number can mean the difference between being accepted into the college of your dreams or having to settle for whichever college will accept you. Your grade point average is the sum of total quality points you have earned at the end of each school year, based on your grades for each class you take. Each letter grade is worth different point values (e.g. "A" = 4 points). These points are added together to determine your grade point average each school year. Most colleges and universities look for students with at least a 3.0 grade point average ("B"), but they will also consider other factors in their selections. Many community colleges will accept students with lower grade point averages but require them to pass their own entrance placement exam. There is normally a fee for this exam. Your current GPA can be found at the bottom of your report card, as well as on your transcript at the end of each school year.

Class Rank

This number is determined by taking your grade point average and comparing it to every student in your graduating class. Your rank tells schools/colleges, prospective employers, military representatives, etc. how competitive your grades are when compared to other students (e.g. – A student who receives straight A's [4.0] throughout his/her high school career will be ranked #1 in the class.) Unless someone else also has straight A's, this student may be the **valedictorian** of his/her graduating class if the rank is maintained. The student with the next highest GPA may be the **salutatorian** of their graduating class if the rank is maintained. (Please refer to your student handbook for more information on this topic.)

Thoughts & Notes:

High School Transcript

Your high school transcript is an up-to-date "snapshot" of every course you have completed since beginning high school. It will also show your final grade for each class, as well as the number of credits earned for each class. Credits are then totaled and recorded at the end of each school year. Freshmen will not have a transcript until the end of their freshman school year after they have earned credits that can be counted toward their graduation requirements.

Your transcript will also show your grade point average (GPA). Some schools will list your class rank on your transcript after you have completed grade 9. Other schools will wait until your junior year to put the class rank on your transcript. Check to see how it is done at your school.

Your transcript is the document that will be reviewed by college admissions officers, as well as potential scholarship sources. Make every effort to maintain at least a 3.5 GPA ("B" average). Some colleges require a higher GPA for admission. You must research this information on each of the colleges you are interested in attending. If you maintain your class rank in the top 15% of your class, you will make yourself a strong candidate to get accepted into a good college as well as to receive scholarships.

Your guidance counselor or the school registrar can get a copy of your transcript for you with advance notice. Some schools may charge you a nominal fee to obtain a copy of your transcript.

*Thoughts & Notes:*_____

Important Stuff Here ✅

More Terms You Need to Know

IB (International Baccalaureate Diploma)

The IB Diploma program is designed as an academically challenging and balanced program of education with final examinations that prepare students for university success and life beyond. The program is normally taught over a two-year period and has gained recognition and respect from the world's leading universities. Visit www.ibo.org/diploma for further information.

Honors Courses/Pre-AP Courses/College Prep

These higher-level courses are designed for students who are prepared for the challenge of higher-level logical and critical thinking skills. The teachers' level of expectation for students enrolled in Honors courses is also higher in that they must be able to work and gain knowledge independently.

College Prep, Honors, and Pre-AP courses typically receive a higher weight of 1.0 added to your GPA. Not only does passing these challenging courses appeal to colleges, but it could also be the determining factor in your class rank. Please consult your guidance counselor for the weights that are applied for these courses in your school district.

AP (Advanced Placement Courses)

These higher-level college preparatory courses are designed to prepare students to successfully pass the AP exam and receive credit toward their college/university of choice. Through these classes, students are expected to strengthen their analytical, critical thinking, and research skills. They must earn a score of at least a "3" to earn college credit for having taken the college-level course during high school. AP courses typically receive a weight of 1.5 added to the GPA (grade point average). Students should visit the College board website at: w.w.w.collegeboard. com for more information on Advanced Placement classes. Consult your guidance counselor for the weights that are applied for these courses in your school district.

PSAT (Pre Standardized Achievement Test)

This is a required pre-test for the SAT that underclassmen take during a pre-scheduled school day. This test is usually administered in the fall. Test scores are used as an indicator to colleges and other organizations regarding students' potential achievement levels in the areas of reading, writing, and math. Ask your counselor about SAT prep courses you can take to better prepare you for the SAT and help improve your scores.

SAT Subject Test (Standardized Achievement Test)

The SAT Subject Tests are one-hour tests that measure knowledge in specific subject areas. Some selective colleges require students to take two or three SAT Subject Tests to be considered for admission or placement. Subjects for consideration include math, foreign languages, biology, etc.

ACT Test (American College Test)

The ACT is a 3-1/2 hour-long multiple-choice test (with the exception of the written essay option) that measures your knowledge in English, math, reading, and science. There is a fee for the ACT. Apply online at www.collegeboard.com. The perfect ACT score is 36.

ASVAB Test (Armed Services Vocational Aptitude Battery)

Military personnel will administer the ASVAB test in the early part of the school year to all students in grade 11. These test results will help you identify your career interests and areas in which you would most likely be successful. Test results will be explained by a representative when they are completed. The test is usually given at the high school on a weekday during school hours. There is no fee for this test.

Scholarships

So, why are we talking about scholarships now? We just entered high school, and college is a long way off.

It's a good idea to start thinking about how you will pay for college as soon as you decide if that is the path you want to take. Believe it or not, once you become involved in high school, you will be amazed at how quickly the next four years are going to fly by. So, we need to make you aware of as much as we can now because it will help you in making your future plans.

Scholarships are another means of providing financial support for college-bound students, even those who will start their journey at a two-year community college. College costs a lot of money, and will discuss ways that you can be prepared to meet that challenge.

Some scholarships are made available to middle school students. For instance, the Ben Carson scholarship. Each year, Dr. Carson accepts scholarship applications from middle school students all over the United States. Students have to meet certain academic requirements and write an essay to be considered for this scholarship and they can apply each year. So, students who are willing to work hard can begin preparing for college right away! See your guidance counselor for more information.

Please view the form on **page 132**. Your scholarship and college admissions deadlines can be organized on one sheet.

At the beginning of your senior year, you will be applying for many, many scholarships. If you have been researching college costs, financial aid, and scholarships before that time, you will be more than prepared to meet the application deadlines and requirements of the scholarships for which you choose to apply.

Thoughts & Notes:

Resumé Development

Do I need a resumé?

A resumé is simply a written summary record of your accomplishments and goals, which you will need for college or employment. Having a resumé ready when you start to apply for your scholarships will be a big help to you. You can begin developing your resumé by keeping track of your accomplishments (academic achievements, sports involvement, volunteer activities, employment, clubs, offices held, etc.). Your parents and counselor will be happy to sit down with you to help you with this task.

Useful information can also be found online by Googling the word "resume" and selecting the format that best fits your needs.

Helpful steps to follow:

Step 1 – Develop a clear and concise educational/ career goal.

Step 2 – List your most recent education completed. Include the school name, address, and grade completed. Use reverse chronological order for each school attended (most recent first). Under education, you may list advanced courses in which you have excelled (e.g. Honors, Advanced Placement).

Step 3 – List employment (most current first). If you have not been employed (received wages for work), proceed to step 4. List the position held, description of duties, and dates for the years you were employed.

Step 4 – List sports activities. Activity, location, position (if applicable), number of year(s) participating.

Step 5 – List club membership/involvement. Name of club, location, office held, number of years involved, description of responsibilities.

Step 6 – References: List the names of at least three (3) persons who could give you a favorable recommendation that includes comments about your character, accomplishments, and goals. OR you could use this phrase at the end of your resumé: Character references upon request.

As you progress in your professional and educational endeavors, your resumé will become more detailed and sophisticated. You may find yourself in need of a curriculum vitae for professional degrees and employment.

Do not be afraid to use your internet connections to research the type of polished resumé you desire. You can also get help with the resumé template in the Microsoft Word program.

Once you complete your resumé and portfolio, they will be useful tools for you throughout your career if you continue to update them regularly.

Sample Student Resumé

Emmanuel L. Whidbee
1 Studious Lane, Bronx, New York 12333
Home: (555)555-5555 • Cell: (566)555-2222
E-mail: Honorstudent@success.com

Education
2020 – 2024
Bronx High School, Bronx, New York

Experience
June 2003 – present: Sales Associate, The Retail Store
- Maintain and restock inventor
- Provide customer service.
- Operate computerized cash register system.

2020 - present: Child Care
- Provide child care for several families after school, weekends, and during school vacations.

Achievements
- National Honor Society: 2020 - 2024
- Academic Honor Roll: 2020 - 2024

Volunteer Experience
- Big Brothers/Big Sisters
- Arlington Literacy Program
- Relay for Life

Interests/Activities
- Member of Bronx High School soccer team
- Boy Scouts
- Piano

Computer Skills
- Proficient with Microsoft Word, Excel, PowerPoint, and Internet

Sample Reference Letter

Furhman Senior High School
080151 Golden Ridge Avenue
Chesapeake, VA 23323
(757) 333-7777 Fax: (757) 333-1212
www.cgwh@highschool.edu
Mr. Alvin R. Mitchell, Principal Mrs. Thelma A. Copes, Vice-Principal

December 1, 2023

Princeton University
Princeton, New Jersey, 08544

Dear Princeton Admissions Representative,

It is with great enthusiasm that I submit this letter of recommendation for one of our most promising students, Jeremiah A. Goodwill. Jeremiah has selected your university as his first choice. We both agree that he would be a perfect fit for your engineering program.

Upon preview of Jeremiah's academic transcript, you will find that he has challenged himself with the most rigorous Advanced Placement and Honors courses we offer. He has maintained at least a 3.98 grade point average throughout his high school career while involving himself in sports, volunteer activities, mentoring, and school life. He proudly represents his school in leadership positions including class president, football captain, and debate team officer. He spends time in his community volunteering in various capacities and spending quality time as a big brother. Jeremiah is honest, respectful and has a genuine regard for helping others.

Jeremiah proudly demonstrates his academic capabilities by earning a combined SAT score of 2350 and an ACT score of 36. He is friendly, outgoing and well-rounded student who is liked by his peers and teachers alike. When you meet with this fine young man, you will agree that he is a special individual that will make his mark on the world and aspire to greatness.

Thank you for your careful consideration of this applicant and the contributions he will bring to your university.

Regards,

Mrs. Sarah Abraham, M. Ed.
Guidance Counselor

Portfolio Development

Do I need a portfolio?

For educational and career purposes, we are defining your high school portfolio as follows: a printed record contained in a three-ring binder that verifies your educational, volunteer, extracurricular, and employment activities you have listed on your resumé. (Your resumé is also included in your portfolio.)

Your portfolio, like your resumé, will grow with you as you accomplish different goals. Even though your resumé and your portfolio are works in progress, they will be very beneficial when you apply for acceptance at various colleges, as well as employment in temporary or career positions.

Your portfolio will be an independent project that will evolve over the next several years. We strongly encourage you to develop the **habit** of keeping track of important documents (like awards and certificates), organizing and labeling them in a notebook, along with developing your resumé, and updating the information as needed. This may give you an advantage over your competition.

The skills of **organization** and **self-discipline** that you will learn while compiling your resumé and portfolio now will be invaluable to you in the future.

> *Don't be afraid of challenges.*
> *Challenges will often push you to your destiny.*

Beginning with grade 9, organize all of your honors, awards, certificates, report cards, and other important documents you have received for that year. (Accomplishments should be grouped by year.) Purchase a three-ring binder with a clear front insert and loads of page protectors.

Your parent, guidance counselor, or English teacher, will be happy to work with you and your adviser to develop your resumé and portfolio. **Represent** yourself and your family well throughout your entire high school career with these indispensable tools!

Thoughts & Notes:

A portfolio is an organized system of documents that verify claims of education, community and sports involvement, volunteerism, academic achievements, and employment. A portfolio is an evolving collection of documents that must be updated frequently as accomplishments are earned.

This user-friendly tracking and organizing system can be used as early as middle school and customized to fit your style and needs. These instructions were developed primarily to help high school and college students get into the habit of saving, documenting, and organizing personal achievements and accomplishments in a portfolio binder.

Once individuals begin this process, they are more likely to continue adding to their portfolios throughout their professional careers.

Get focused
Get busy
Get organized!

Thoughts & Notes:

Important Stuff Here ✓

What can I put in my portfolio

1. Report cards and progress report

2. Sports and club involvement – offices held, awards, pictures

3. Volunteer activity – verifying documents, pictures

4. Copies of standardized test results

5. Employment

6. Resume

Items to purchase for the project:

1. 2" or 3" presentation binder – your color choice

2. Approximately 50 clear page protectors (to get started)

3. 1 pack of tab dividers

Organizing Information

1. Gather all of your documents.

2. Sort documents into similar categories by year (most recent on top).

3. Label divider sections accordingly (e.g. report cards, sports/clubs, volunteer activities).

4. Place documents in the appropriate labeled sections, with one document per page protector. If you choose to use two documents per page protector, be sure to turn the documents back-to-back so the front is in full view on both sides.

Binder Set-Up

1. The front cover of the binder can be personalized with a design and personal information.

2. Fill binder with page protectors.

3. Insert dividers according to the determined number of categories in which you have separated similar documents.

Portfolio Maintenance

1. As you continue to earn awards and certificates, make sure you keep copies of them for your portfolio.

2. Whenever possible, include a picture or two that captures your noteworthy events.

3. Updating your portfolio is a good project to work on during planned and uninterrupted time.

4. To maintain a good, usable portfolio, update it often.

Students...

It is extremely important for you to have good study habits and organizational skills. If you have been accustomed to doing your homework while watching TV, texting, talking on the phone, or listening to music, it's time to make some positive changes. We want you to develop skills that you will need both now and in the future, not only for college but for your entire life.

Study Tips & Organizing Strategies That Work:

1. Schedule specific times to study subject material every day using an agenda book, planner, or organizer. Studying whenever new information is presented helps you to utilize it when problem-solving and preparing for tests. Developing strong study habits and making studying a part of your daily routine will help you to be properly prepared for tests, eliminating the need for cramming.

2. Write your assignments down as soon as you get them. Check them off your list individually upon completion.

3. DO NOT PROCRASTINATE! Putting off the completion of your work just wastes time, makes you feel guilty, and causes you to do sloppy work at the last minute. If you pace yourself, you will feel great and get the work done on time!

4. Take good notes and/or record (voice record only) the classroom sessions.

5. Tackle the big assignments first, but break them up into sections so you do not overwhelm yourself. Check off items as they are completed.

6. Make sure you keep all information for each class in the same place—either a binder or notebook. Keep your notebook and backpack neat and organized so that your information is easily accessible.

7. Turn assignments in on time!

8. Begin a study group with other students. Be careful, though, that the work gets done and your time is not wasted.

9. Don't be afraid to ask questions and get clarification about any information you don't understand while the questions are still fresh in your mind.

10. Ask your parents to help you. They can ask you questions about your study material, and then you can respond verbally or in writing. This is an excellent practice to help you learn the material.

11. Use your time wisely. If you are involved in sports or extracurricular activities, you'll have to balance your time to satisfy all of your commitments.

FRESHM
FRES
FRE
F

AN

MAN

SHMAN

RESHMA

FRESHMAN

Freshman Academic & Goal Planning

Here you are, about to step into a whole new academic experience. Your freshman year of high school can be very challenging. You may be an underclassman, but you can still make a real difference in the next four years. Oftentimes, you are in a much larger environment with new teachers that you have to build a relationship with, along with lots of new students that you do not know. Even though some of your friends from middle school have transitioned into different high schools, you will make new and lasting friendships during the next four years. Instead of approaching this challenge with dread, look at it as a wonderful opportunity to grow and learn.

It may take a week or so to adjust to the "newness" of high school, but you will settle into a comfortable routine in no time. After you have gauged the amount of time it takes to navigate from one classroom to the next before the late bell rings, figured out your locker combination, gotten over the embarrassment of changing for gym, and decided whether or not you are going to eat the cafeteria food, you will find that high school life is pretty cool.

Important Stuff Here ✅

Remember these tips:

- Get to know your guidance counselor. Take the opportunity to introduce yourself and ask lots of questions about the educational process. Your counselor and parents should be included in your course selection process.

- Make every attempt to maintain a 3.0 Grade Point Average (GPA) or above. (You'll soon find it easy to begin thinking in terms of GPA instead of A's and B's.)

- Take electives that interest you. This may include academic as well as non-academic classes that you can earn credit for passing. These courses may just lead to a career pathway or college major.

- Join a club or sports team. Get involved in school life! Those who put more effort into their high school experience get more out of it.

- Keep track of awards, recognitions, volunteer hours, and other documentation for your resumé and portfolio.

- Develop a success strategy that works for you.

Freshman class dues – Amounts vary from school to school. Contact the freshman class adviser.

Thoughts & Notes:

I need to get
ORGANIZED!

Please use a check for those areas where you need to improve. Being organized in all areas of your life reduces stress and anxiety while allowing you to get things done! What a great feeling!!

☐ I have a separate notebook for each of my classes.

☐ Class notes and other material are kept together for studying purposes.

☐ I have a specific place in my notebook for writing down homework assignments.

☐ My backpack is neat and organized.

☐ I make good use of my time by keeping it organized.

☐ I prepare for school the night before.

☐ I make sure I have all of the tools required to pass my class.

☐ My study area at home is clean, quiet, and well-lit.

☐ I do not put off until tomorrow what I should be doing today.

☐ I ask for help when I need it.

☐ I include my parents in my plans and decisions.

☐ I arrive at school early, take care of my needs, and get to class on time.

Signature: _____ Date: _____

Important Stuff Here ✔️

Good Study Habits Are a Must!

☐ I have a set time to study each day.

☐ I have a place to study that is quiet and well-lit.

☐ I review my notes from class when I get home from school. This helps me to be better prepared for tests and quizzes.

☐ My homework is my priority.

☐ I turn my homework in on time or early because I am prepared.

☐ I divide my class projects into sections and complete them ahead of time to improve my chances of getting a good grade.

☐ When I am absent from school, I ensure that I obtain missed assignments and complete them on time.

☐ I make it a practice to stay after school for make-up work or get extra help on work that I don't understand.

Signature: _____ Date: _____

Freshman Grade Tracking Sheet

Enter the grade you earn in each of your classes for each semester. Keep a copy of your final report card at the end of each school year and include it in your portfolio.

Course	1st Quarter	2nd Quarter	Mid-Term*	3rd Quarter	4th Quarter	Final Grade	Credit Earned

Include classes you may be taking through programs such as Academic Challenge, Credit Recovery, etc.

Quarters I made honor roll: ____1st ____2nd ____3rd ____4th

Will I be eligible to join the National Honor Society next year? ___Yes ___No

End-of-year Grade Point Average (GPA): _____

End-of-year class rank: _____

Awards & Honors:

_____

_____

*See page 62 for **Mid-Term Check-Up**: a space you can identify classes where you need help and can proactively plan your success.

My Freshman Academic Goals

Your goals may change as you mature and experience life. This is perfectly normal!

Short-Term Goals	Plan of Action to achieve Goal	Date Goal Achieved

goals!

Long-Term Goals	Plan of Action to achieve Goal	Date Goal Achieved

My Freshman Career Goals

Short-Term Goals	Plan of Action to achieve Goal	Date Goal Achieved

goals!

Long-Term Goals	Plan of Action to achieve Goal	Date Goal Achieved

Colleges of Interest

Start researching colleges early. The sooner, the better!

College Name	Location	Website	Cost Per Year	Date Visited Campus

Thoughts & Notes:

Careers of Interest

The earlier you begin researching a career, the more useful information you will find to help with you decision.

Career Title	Education Required	Salary Range	States with Best Salary	Research Completed Date

Thoughts & Notes:

Mid-Term Check-Up

Class I need help with:	Date	Current Grade	Plan of Action	Date Achieved	New Grade

Thoughts & Notes:

Thoughts & Notes:

I will do everything in my power to maximize my potential in every area of my life!

SOPHO

SOPHO

SOP

S

MORE

MORE

HOMOR

OPHOMO

SOPHOMORE

Sophomore Academic & Goal Planning

As a sophomore, you are still an underclassman, but you have risen up a notch on the school ladder. You should feel more confident and better able to navigate high school.

The school you attend might offer driver's education to sophomores. The privilege of taking that class comes with major responsibilities. Some schools will not allow you to take the class if you are failing a major subject, such as English. The prospect of getting a driver's license should be an incentive to improve your performance in all areas.

If you didn't get a chance to meet your school counselor as a freshman, it's important to make a personal visit to their office as soon as possible. To do so, you'll need to get a pass from your teacher and make an appointment with the counselor. Your counselor can help you identify which career path best fits your academic and personal interests, as well as your aptitudes. So don't hesitate to reach out for guidance and support!

This year, you may want to think about finding a summer job. Work permits are available in the high school office. Additionally, it's a good idea to take the SAT or ACT test. You can check with your guidance counselor for more information.

Continue to meet new friends and involve yourself in extra-curricular activities and volunteer work. Mentoring younger students is a great way to give back to your community! Your local Boys & Girls Club is looking for bright, young leaders just like you!

Remember these tips:

- Visit www.collegeboard.com to register to take the SAT or www.act.org for the ACT.

- If you have not already done so, purchase a binder and page protectors for your portfolio, and begin organizing it by sections according to awards, report cards, etc. (See pages 36-42)

- Begin working on your resumé if you have not done so already.

- Your school counselor and parents should be included in your course selection process each year.

- Attend local college/career fairs and financial aid nights. Information should be available in your guidance office or visit www.EducationPlanner.org.

- Review and revise your success strategy.

Sophomore class dues – Amounts vary from school to school. Contact the sophomore class adviser.

Students:

If your school offers driver's education, you will likely be driving your parent's vehicle. However, it's important to consider the various costs associated with driving, such as gas, insurance, and repairs. To offset these costs, you may want to consider getting a part-time job.

You can obtain a work permit from the school guidance office to help you get started. It's worth noting that having a part-time job will also look impressive on your resumé.

71

I need to get ORGANIZED!

Please use a check for those areas where you need to improve. Being organized in all areas of your life reduces stress and anxiety while allowing you to get things done! What a great feeling!!

☐ I have a separate notebook for each of my classes.

☐ Class notes and other material are kept together for studying purposes.

☐ I have a specific place in my notebook for writing down homework assignments.

☐ My backpack is neat and organized.

☐ I make good use of my time by keeping it organized.

☐ I prepare for school the night before.

☐ I make sure I have all of the tools required to pass my class.

☐ My study area at home is clean, quiet, and well-lit.

☐ I do not put off until tomorrow what I should be doing today.

☐ I ask for help when I need it.

☐ I include my parents in my plans and decisions.

☐ I arrive at school early, take care of my needs, and get to class on time.

Signature: _____ Date: _____

Important Stuff Here ✔️

Good Study Habits Are a Must!

☐ I have a set time to study each day.

☐ I have a place to study that is quiet and well-lit.

☐ I review my notes from class when I get home from school. This helps me to be better prepared for tests and quizzes.

☐ My homework is my priority.

☐ I turn my homework in on time or early because I am prepared.

☐ I divide my class projects into sections and complete them ahead of time to improve my chances of getting a good grade.

☐ When I am absent from school, I ensure that I obtain missed assignments and complete them on time.

☐ I make it a practice to stay after school for make-up work or get extra help on work that I don't understand.

Signature: _____ Date: _____

Sophomore Grade Tracking Sheet

Enter the grade you earn in each of your classes for each semester. Keep a copy of your final report card at the end of each school year and include it in your portfolio.

Course	1st Quarter	2nd Quarter	Mid-Term*	3rd Quarter	4th Quarter	Final Grade	Credit Earned

Include classes you may be taking through programs such as Academic Challenge, Credit Recovery, etc.

Quarters I made honor roll: ____1st ____2nd ____3rd ____4th

Will I be eligible to join the National Honor Society next year? ___Yes ___No

End-of-year Grade Point Average (GPA): _____

End-of-year class rank: _____

Awards & Honors:

_____

_____

*See page 84 for **Mid-Term Check-Up**: a space you can identify classes where you need help and can proactively plan your success.

My Sophomore Academic Goals

Your goals may change as you mature and experience life. This is perfectly normal!

Short-Term Goals	Plan of Action to achieve Goal	Date Goal Achieved

goals!

Long-Term Goals	Plan of Action to achieve Goal	Date Goal Achieved

My Sophomore Career Goals

Short-Term Goals	Plan of Action to achieve Goal	Date Goal Achieved

goals!

Long-Term Goals	Plan of Action to achieve Goal	Date Goal Achieved

Colleges of Interest

Start researching colleges early. The sooner, the better!

SOPHOMORE

College Name	Location	Website	Cost Per Year	Date Visited Campus

*Thoughts & Notes:*_____

SOPHOMORE

Careers of Interest

The earlier you begin researching a career, the more useful information you will find to help with you decision.

SOPHOMORE

Career Title	Education Required	Salary Range	States with Best Salary	Research Completed Date

Thoughts & Notes:

Sophomore Test Tracking

Test	Date	Reading Score	Writing Score	Math Score	English Score	Science Score	Subject Test	Total Scores
ACT								
PSAT								
ASVAB								

Thoughts & Notes:

Thoughts & Notes: _____

SOPHOMORE

Mid-Term Check-Up

Class I need help with:	Date	Current Grade	Plan of Action	Date Achieved	New Grade

Thoughts & Notes:

SOPHOMORE

Thoughts & Notes:_____

I will do everything in my power to maximize my potential in every area of my life!

JUNIOR

JUNIO

JU

R

NIOR

JUNIOR

JUNIOR

Junior Academic & Goal Planning

You reached the status of "upperclassman"! Congratulations!

If you have not already taken a college entrance exam (SAT, ACT), now is a good time to complete the online application on www.collegeboard.com and www.act.org. The approximate cost of the exams is sixty dollars ($60) per test. The cost will vary for each test, be sure to check the test's website or with your guidance counselor to confirm the fee or how to make a payment (online or by check).

Visit your guidance counselor to determine whether or not you are eligible for a fee waiver to compensate you for this cost.

- If you plan to enlist in the military, your ASVAB test scores are very important. Contact a local recruiting office for more information.

- Stay focused. Make sure you maintain your GPA, and make improvements as needed.

- End your junior year with a strong grade point average! A representative from the colleges and scholarships you apply to will be using your GPA from the end of your junior year in their evaluation process.

- Your resumé and portfolio should be shaping up now. You have two years' worth of accomplishments to record and organize.

- Your grades, course selections, and college choices should be discussed at length with your school counselor. Make sure you are on track for graduation and are meeting all of the requirements

- Stay involved. Volunteer or mentor in your community.

- Strengthen your success strategy. Revise if needed.

Asking the following questions will help with the selection process:

1. Does this college offer my major?

2. Am I satisfied with the location?

3. Can I afford to attend this school?

4. Would I benefit more from attending a two-year junior college and then transferring to a four-year university?

As you begin your research, other questions will be generated that you should find answers to in order to make an informed decision.

Junior class dues - Amounts vary from school to school. Contact the junior class adviser.

Students:

There may be a big pull on the family purse strings in your junior year if you decide to participate in homecoming events and the prom. Some students also want to purchase their class ring during their junior year. These are decisions the family should make together. It would greatly benefit you to be responsible for sharing in the cost of these privileges if you will be participating.

The junior year is also a good time to begin scheduling college visits. Save yourself time and money by only visiting those colleges that offer the major you are interested in studying. College visits should be planned for vacation times, the winter or spring break, or during the summer.

Visit www.EducationPlanner.org for help.

I need to get ORGANIZED!

Please use a check for those areas where you need to improve. Being organized in all areas of your life reduces stress and anxiety while allowing you to get things done! What a great feeling!!

JUNIOR

☐ I have a separate notebook for each of my classes.

☐ Class notes and other material are kept together for studying purposes.

☐ I have a specific place in my notebook for writing down homework assignments.

☐ My backpack is neat and organized.

☐ I make good use of my time by keeping it organized.

☐ I prepare for school the night before.

☐ I make sure I have all of the tools required to pass my class.

☐ My study area at home is clean, quiet, and well-lit.

☐ I do not put off until tomorrow what I should be doing today.

☐ I ask for help when I need it.

☐ I include my parents in my plans and decisions.

☐ I arrive at school early, take care of my needs, and get to class on time.

J U N I O R

Signature: _____ Date: _____

Important Stuff Here ✔

Good Study Habits Are a Must!

☐ I have a set time to study each day.

☐ I have a place to study that is quiet and well-lit.

☐ I review my notes from class when I get home from school. This helps me to be better prepared for tests and quizzes.

☐ My homework is my priority.

☐ I turn my homework in on time or early because I am prepared.

☐ I divide my class projects into sections and complete them ahead of time to improve my chances of getting a good grade.

☐ When I am absent from school, I ensure that I obtain missed assignments and complete them on time.

☐ I make it a practice to stay after school for make-up work or get extra help on work that I don't understand.

Signature: _____ Date: _____

Junior Grade Tracking Sheet

Enter the grade you earn in each of your classes for each semester. Keep a copy of your final report card at the end of each school year and include it in your portfolio.

Course	1st Quarter	2nd Quarter	Mid-Term*	3rd Quarter	4th Quarter	Final Grade	Credit Earned

Include classes you may be taking through programs such as Academic Challenge, Credit Recovery, etc.

Quarters I made honor roll: _____1st _____2nd _____3rd _____4th

Will I be eligible to join the National Honor Society next year? ___Yes ___No

End-of-year Grade Point Average (GPA): _____

End-of-year class rank: _____

Awards & Honors:

_____

_____

*See page 106 for **Mid-Term Check-Up**: a space you can identify classes where you need help and can proactively plan your success.

My Junior Academic Goals

Your goals may change as you mature and experience life. This is perfectly normal!

Short-Term Goals	Plan of Action to achieve Goal	Date Goal Achieved

goals!

Long-Term Goals	Plan of Action to achieve Goal	Date Goal Achieved

My Junior Career Goals

Short-Term Goals	Plan of Action to achieve Goal	Date Goal Achieved

goals!

Long-Term Goals	Plan of Action to achieve Goal	Date Goal Achieved

Colleges of Interest

Start researching colleges early. The sooner, the better!

College Name	Location	Website	Cost Per Year	Date Visited Campus

Thoughts & Notes:

JUNIOR

Careers of Interest

The earlier you begin researching a career, the more useful information you will find to help with you decision.

Career Title	Education Required	Salary Range	States with Best Salary	Research Completed Date

Thoughts & Notes:

Junior Test Tracking

Test	Date	Reading Score	Writing Score	Math Score	English Score	Science Score	Subject Test	Total Scores
ACT								
PSAT								
ASVAB								
SAT								
SAT Subject								
SAT Subject								

Thoughts & Notes:

Thoughts & Notes:

JUNIOR

Mid-Term Check-Up

Class I need help with:	Date	Current Grade	Plan of Action	Date Achieved	New Grade

Thoughts & Notes:

Thoughts & Notes:

JUNIO

I will do everything in my power to maximize my potential in every area of my life!

SENIOR

SENIO

S

R

ENIOR

SENIOR

SENIOR

Senior Academic & Goal Planning

Well, it is finally here! You are a proud high school Senior and a true upperclassman. Graduation is within reach. Congratulations, Senior!

It is vital that you meet one-on-one with your counselor early in the fall to discuss your plans for college, the military, technical school, or the transition to the workplace.

Get a copy of your transcript from your guidance counselor. *You will need the information contained in this document to apply for scholarships and colleges.*

When you apply for colleges and scholarships, you will need to submit letters of recommendation from your teachers, counselor, coach, or administrators. To ensure that the letter is specific to your achievements and academic record, make sure you provide the person with a copy of your resumé and information regarding the scholarship or college where you are applying. Additionally, when requesting official transcripts from your guidance office, it is recommended to ask for several at once so that you have them available when needed.

If your SAT or ACT scores are not as high as you would like, take the tests again in the early fall to improve your scores before you apply to college. If you have challenged yourself with AP classes, consider taking the AP exams. Discuss this with your guidance counselor and parents first.

Important Stuff Here ✔️

Remember these tips:

- As you begin your application process to colleges, financial aid sources, the military, or employment, be aware that your e-mail address should not contain any negative or suggestive overtones. Likewise, the content of your social media pages represents your character and integrity. Make sure you send the right message, especially to those who are making decisions about your future.

- Stay focused and organized. Update your portfolio and polish your resumé. Check them thoroughly for errors.

- Some scholarships require a personal essay. After completing the essay, ask at least one other person to proofread it for you.

- Keep track of all deadlines, and adhere to them religiously.

- Make copies of all information you submit to colleges and financial aid resources.

- Attend college fairs and financial aid workshops. Talk to reps from the colleges you are considering. Research at www.EducationPlanner.org.

- To find the best fit for your interests and abilities, make sure you read the mission statement of the college prior to applying. You'll want to look at more than the degree programs they offer to be sure extra-curricular activities, location, cost, size of the campus and student body, and other aspects fit your preferences.

- Access virtual college tours online; this will allow you to see the campus as well as help narrow down your selection choices before deciding on visits.

- Apply for financial aid at www.fafsa.edu.gov as soon as possible (after January 1st).

- Apply for every possible scholarship for which you are eligible, even though financial aid probably will not pay for all of your college costs. Your goal is to maintain a GPA of 3.5 or above in your senior year to better your chances of being offered financial assistance that does not have to be repaid. (Contact the college bursar's office about stipulations to these funds.)

- Take your portfolio along with you for interviews with college admissions representatives, scholarship representatives, recruiters, or prospective employers.

- Review and revise your success strategy for college.

Senior class dues – Amounts vary from school to school. Contact the senior class adviser. These dues are very important because they will not only be used for your senior prom but also to establish a fund that can be used in the future for class reunions.

Students:

Congratulations on a job well done!

Things to consider for your Senior Year:

- Purchasing senior and graduation items will require large sums of money.

- All class dues need to be paid in full prior to graduation.

- Cap and gown packages can be ordered from your school or online. Packets can include announcements, tassels, portraits, and other items. Contact the senior class adviser for specifics.

- Class rings and yearbooks may be purchased.

- You might be expected to pay for homecoming, the prom, and senior week if you and your family decide that you have earned the privilege to attend.

Thoughts & Notes:

I need to get ORGANIZED!

Please use a check for those areas where you need to improve. Being organized in all areas of your life reduces stress and anxiety while allowing you to get things done! What a great feeling!!

- ☐ I have a separate notebook for each of my classes.
- ☐ Class notes and other material are kept together for studying purposes.
- ☐ I have a specific place in my notebook for writing down homework assignments.
- ☐ My backpack is neat and organized.
- ☐ I make good use of my time by keeping it organized.
- ☐ I prepare for school the night before.
- ☐ I make sure I have all of the tools required to pass my class.
- ☐ My study area at home is clean, quiet, and well-lit.
- ☐ I do not put off until tomorrow what I should be doing today.
- ☐ I ask for help when I need it.
- ☐ I include my parents in my plans and decisions.
- ☐ I arrive at school early, take care of my needs, and get to class on time.

Signature: _____ Date: _____

SENIOR

Important Stuff Here ✔️

Good Study Habits Are a Must!

- ☐ I have a set time to study each day.

- ☐ I have a place to study that is quiet and well-lit.

- ☐ I review my notes from class when I get home from school. This helps me to be better prepared for tests and quizzes.

- ☐ My homework is my priority.

- ☐ I turn my homework in on time or early because I am prepared.

- ☐ I divide my class projects into sections and complete them ahead of time to improve my chances of getting a good grade.

- ☐ When I am absent from school, I ensure that I obtain missed assignments and complete them on time.

- ☐ I make it a practice to stay after school for make-up work or get extra help on work that I don't understand.

Signature: _____ Date: _____

Senior Grade Tracking Sheet

Enter the grade you earn in each of your classes for each semester. Keep a copy of your final report card at the end of each school year and include it in your portfolio.

Course	1st Quarter	2nd Quarter	Mid-Term*	3rd Quarter	4th Quarter	Final Grade	Credit Earned

Include classes you may be taking through programs such as Academic Challenge, Credit Recovery, etc.

Quarters I made honor roll: ____1st ____2nd ____3rd ____4th

Will I be eligible to join the National Honor Society next year? ___Yes ___No

End-of-year Grade Point Average (GPA): _____

End-of-year class rank: _____

Awards & Honors:

_____

_____

*See page 130 for **Mid-Term Check-Up**: a space you can identify classes where you need help and can proactively plan your success.

S
E
N
I
O
R

My Senior Academic Goals

Your goals may change as you mature and experience life. This is perfectly normal!

Short-Term Goals	Plan of Action to achieve Goal	Date Goal Achieved

goals!

Long-Term Goals	Plan of Action to achieve Goal	Date Goal Achieved

My Senior Career Goals

Short-Term Goals	Plan of Action to achieve Goal	Date Goal Achieved

goals!

Long-Term Goals	Plan of Action to achieve Goal	Date Goal Achieved

Colleges of Interest

Start researching colleges early. The sooner, the better!

College Name	Location	Website	Cost Per Year	Date Visited Campus

Thoughts & Notes:

Careers of Interest

The earlier you begin researching a career, the more useful information you will find to help with you decision.

Career Title	Education Required	Salary Range	States with Best Salary	Research Completed Date

Thoughts & Notes:

Senior Test Tracking

Test	Date	Reading Score	Writing Score	Math Score	English Score	Science Score	Subject Test	Total Scores
ACT								
ASVAB								
SAT								
SAT Subject								
SAT Subject								

Thoughts & Notes:

Thoughts & Notes:

Mid-Term Check-Up

Class I need help with:	Date	Current Grade	Plan of Action	Date Achieved	New Grade

Thoughts & Notes:

College & Scholarship Application Deadline Tracking Sheet

Date	October — Applicaton	✓	Date	November — Applicaton	✓	Date	December — Applicaton	✓

Date	January — Applicaton	✓	Date	February — Applicaton	✓	Date	March — Applicaton	✓

Date	April — Applicaton	✓	Date	May — Applicaton	✓	Date	June — Applicaton	✓

SENIOR

Important Stuff Here ✔

Thoughts & Notes:

College Acceptances

College Name	Date Accepted	Location	Cost Per Year	Acceptance Decision Deadline	Yes? No?

Thoughts & Notes:

Scholarships Received

Name of Scholarship	Amount Received	Method of Acceptance	Date Scholarship Sent to College

Thoughts & Notes:

Preparation for Your
First Year of College

Checklist of Helpful Information

Once you have selected the college you wish to attend and have received your letter of acceptance, make sure you follow the freshman "To Do" list supplied by your college.

This list will contain everything you need to survive your first year. <u>Do not make any purchases until you review your list thoroughly.</u>

*Thoughts & Notes:*_____

Important Stuff Here ✓

Here are some other tips that will come in handy:

- Visit your dorm room; don't just rely on website pictures. Most rooms are smaller than they appear online, so you don't want to run the risk of purchasing and packing too many items that will not fit in your allotted space.

- Depending on how far your college is from home and how frequently you will be able to get home, pack the type of clothing you will need for the season. You can switch clothing during visits home so you will not use more than your allotted space in your dorm room.

- If you choose to live in the dorm, make sure that you meet your roommate(s) before you move in. A face-to-face meeting is always best, but at least have conversations over the telephone to get to know one another before moving in together.

- Make sure you track the amount of fees and deposits you have to make that are not covered by financial aid, such as room deposits and admission fees.

- Meet and form a good relationship with the residential adviser (RA) of your dorm. That person will share valuable information with you to help make your transition to independent college life easier.

S E N I O R

- Attend as many freshman activities offered by your school as possible, even if they are not mandatory. This will help you to meet new people, as well as open doors of opportunity to participate in activities on and off campus.

- A laptop and printer are a must-have for college students.

- Some colleges allow freshman students to have their cars on campus. There is a parking fee attached to this privilege.

- After registering for your freshman college classes and receiving your course syllabus, do some price comparisons before purchasing your books. All you need is the book title, author, and ISBN. Used books may be available in your college bookstore. You can also rent books much cheaper at www.chegg.com or do comparative shopping at www.ecampus.com.

Students:

If you choose to live on campus, it is quite common to experience homesickness. However, it is completely normal and nothing to worry about. Your parents can help you cope with care packages, letters, phone calls, or texts to check on how you're doing. Although change can be difficult, it's important to embrace it. It's okay to express to your loved ones that you miss them and even tell them when you need their support. It takes courage to ask for help when you need it.

Important Things
You Need to Know About Getting
Into the College of Your Choice

Early Decision/Early Action

Early decision simply means that you apply early and receive the college's acceptance or rejection decision early. Some colleges offer this option, but you must be aware of your responsibilities if you choose this option:

If you are **accepted** as an early decision applicant, you *must attend that school.* The early acceptance decision is **binding**. Even if you are offered a better financial aid package by another school, *you cannot accept it.*

Early Action is non-binding but works pretty much the same way as early decision. Choose the option that best fits your needs. These are the types of discussions that need to happen with your family

About Scholarships

You have to make sure that your college receives all of your scholarship awards. Check-in with your financial aid office to make sure the money has been credited to your account. If not, you need to contact the source that awarded the scholarship to you and follow up on making to make sure it is sent to your school.

Important Stuff Here ✓

If you make a room deposit to a college that you decide not to attend, don't forget to **get your refund!**

Take advantage of freshman orientation sessions and new student programs and activities. Participating in these programs will help acclimate you to college life.

College On-Line

This is a viable option for students who desire to earn a degree but wish to do so from the comforts of their own home (for whatever reason). College online gives the student more flexibility. One of the advantages is that you won't have to be concerned about dorm fees and other costs associated with living on campus. One of the disadvantages is that you will not enjoy the experience of connecting and interacting with people from near and far.

Make copies of everything you send to colleges. Information sometimes gets lost in the mail!

Make sure at least one other set of eyes edits your application and essays before submitting them to colleges. You do not want your application to be tossed for simple mistakes and spelling errors.

Personally Speaking

- Make sure you have your physical and that your medical records are up to date

  - Find a pharmacy near your campus
- Take care of your dental and eye appointments
- Find out which banks have free ATMs on campus. Think about opening an account with that bank for your convenience and to avoid charges. Make sure your parents have plenty of deposit slips in case they need to deposit money for your access.
- Many banks offer credit cards to college students. They just send it through the mail with your name on it without you ever having to apply. AVOID THE TEMPTATION TO USE IT LIKE THE PLAGUE! CUT IT UP IMMEDIATELY!

What You Will Need to Survive in the Dorm

Dorm rooms are only so big so don't over-shop and waste money. Before you start shopping for your dorm room, make sure to check with your college about the list of items that you need to purchase. However, below is a list of items that may appear on your list and give you an idea of what you will need:

- Bed: 2 sets of extra long twin sheets; blankets/comforter, pillows, mattress pad

- Bath: Towels, washcloths, toothbrush and toothpaste, shower shoes, shampoo and conditioner, hair clippers, hair dryer, portable caddie, comb and brush, body wash.

- Furniture: Desk lamp, wastebasket, full-length mirror, Desk chair, comfortable chair or floor pillows, television.

- Desk Supplies: envelopes, stamps, calculator, calendar, bulletin board, laptop, planner

- Miscellaneous: batteries, alarm clock, first aid kit, hangers, surge protector, dishes, silverware, plastic storage containers, flashlight, iron, ironing board, food storage containers, vacuum, sanitizing agents, microwave food, snacks, and drinks.

- Storage: Plastic storage containers with lids (under the bed and storage for kitchen items). Some dorm rooms come equipped with a refrigerator and microwave.

Here is advice for your to follow during your collegiate career:

- Properly allocate time towards schoolwork and extra-curriculars.

- Always be prepared for the future and stay ahead of coursework.

- Maintain a balanced and healthy diet. Eating right can help you focus better and lessen stress.

- Talk to your professors if you're having trouble with coursework. Many offer office hours to those who need assistance.

- There may be opportunities on campus for additional financial assistance if needed. There may be jobs, programs, or scholarships that can help cover some of tuition or expenses.

Important Stuff Here ✔

- Sit at the front of the class, this will help you focus during lectures. It is likely the professor will also notice you more and it can affect your grade.

- Find a quiet and non-distracting environment to study. The library is a great place to get work done.

- Getting enough sleep is very important. Lectures can sometimes be lengthy and it's easy to drift off if you're not getting quality rest.

- Study thoroughly for midterms and finals; they generally carry a lot of weight towards the final grade.

- Get to know your advisor. They can help with questions you have and can help navigate scheduling classes and working towards your educational and career goals.

S
E
N
I
O
R

College Cost Considerations

These are thoughts for you to consider when applying for colleges and to weigh the costs of expenses that may not be built into the up-front cost of college.

- Tuition for in-state vs. out-of-state vs. online institutions

- Buy new vs. old vs. renting textbooks

- Live on campus vs. rent an apartment vs. commuting from home

- Is there a fee to have a car on campus?

- Can I change roommates?

- How do I get a full ride for college?

- How do I find out about internship opportunities?

- Can I study abroad?

Important Stuff Here ✅

Time Management Tips

- Properly managing time is unarguably the most important skill you will need to thrive in college.

- Buy an agenda book or manage a virtual calendar to keep track of important dates and deadlines for exams, essays, projects, and meetings.

- Attack assignments and other responsibilities proactively. If you start early, you won't have to work as hard.

- Develop a schedule for how to allocate your time and stick to it.

- Prioritize the tasks that are the most important at the time.

- Make a daily to-do list to help organize thoughts and complete tasks.

I wish I had known...

Advice from college students and alumni from various universities to share thoughts they wish they knew before enrolling:

> I wish I had known
> to make sure to go to all of my classes. I skipped quite a few lectures my first semester and it definitely hurt my GPA.

> I wish I had known
> to be more sociable and go to campus activities.

> I definitely wish I had asked my fellow students about which professors to take for classes. You want professors that are fair and have a passion for sharing knowledge of their field.

I wish I had looked for more summer internship opportunities. They are generally positive (and paid!) experiences that look great on resumes and CVs.

I wish I had known how to take college more seriously and study harder. College takes a lot more focus and persistence than high school.

Choose your friends wisely. College is one of the best experiences of your life. Make sure you see it through with people that really care about you.

Thoughts & Notes:

I will do everything in my power to maximize my potential in every area of my life!

SENIOR

Thoughts & Notes:_____

Thoughts & Notes:

"It is the responsibility of every adult to make sure that children hear what we have learned from the lessons of life and to hear over and over that we love them and that they are not alone."

— Marian Wright Edelman

Lawyer, Educator, Children's Advocate, First African-American Woman admitted to the Mississippi State Bar

Important Stuff Here ✅

Useful Websites

Take the opportunity to visit your school guidance counselor for scholarship information. These sites will only get you started on your search for money to pay for college tuition.

College Searches / PSAT / NMSQT – SAT & AP Scores
www.collegeboard.org

College and Financial Aid Information
www.fastweb.com

Free Financial Aid Application
studentaid.gov

Scholarship and Financial Aid Search
www.scholarshipowl.com

Virtual Campus Tours
 www.campustours.com

College Planning
www.petersons.com

Scholarship Search for High School Seniors
www.collegenet.com

S
E
N
I
O
R

United Negro College Fund
www.uncf.org
College Majors, SAT, Scholarships
www.princetonreview.com

Saving for College
www.collegesavings.org

Government Financial Aid/Grants/Loans
www2.ed.gov/finaid

Smart Guide to Financial Aid
finaid.org

Plan/Finance Education/Career Development
career.iresearchnet.com

American Council on Education
collegepossible.org

Free No Essay Scholarships
www.niche.com/students with disabilities
smartcollege.org

Scholarship Compendium
scholarships.delawarestudentsuccess.org

Two Queen Beas Scholarship
www.arkeducation.org

Simmons Memorial Foundation
www.smfnonprofit.org
Decoding Financial Aid Award Letters
collegeaidpro.com

How to Read Your Financial Aid Award Letters
scholarships360.org

Academic Book Rentals
www.chegg.com

Explore Military Options and Career Opportunities
www.asvabprogram.com

Identify College Majors and Narrow Your Career Search
www.mymajors.com

Free SAT Preparation Site
www.number2.com

NCAA Eligibility Center for Student Athletes
web3.ncaa.org/ecwr3

Hispanic Association of Colleges and Universities
www.hacu.net

Minority Scholarship Resource Links
www.scholarships.com
www.collegescholarships.org/financial-aid

Hispanic Heritage Foundation
hispanicheritage.org
Latino College Dollars
www.hsf.net

Ruby's Rainbow
rubysrainbow.org/scholarship-application

Study Abroad
studyabroad.state.gov

Special Needs Scholarship
www.stepupforstudents.org

International Students Scholarships: See College
Financial Aid Officer

Thoughts & Notes:

161

About the Author

Joyce Sessoms has always known that helping people plays a major role in her purpose on earth.

Her early professional life included serving as a social worker / advocate for battered women and an HIV/AIDS Case Manager. She later pursued her love for all things education and served for 10 years as a school counselor until her first retirement. Her accomplishments include an Associate in Applied Science, a Bachelor's in Behavioral Science, a Bachelor's in Biblical Studies, and a Masters in Education.

Sensing an urgency to help students on a more individual basis, she and her husband, Furman, with God's guidance and instruction, founded The ARK Educational Resource Center After-School Tutoring Program.

This non-profit has grown to provide not only one-on-one tutoring in math and reading for K-12 students, but mentoring groups for teen boys & teen girls, a parent group, and a sound engineering technology program.

High School Grand Slam Student/Parent Edition is another way of reaching and providing help to students who may otherwise miss out on a productive education and fulfilling career.

Mrs. Sessoms believes, as the late Marva Collins lived and taught, that, "There is a brilliant child locked inside every student."

The Sessoms are the proud parents of three, grandparents of seven, and great-grandparents of six beautiful and intelligent blessings.

www.ingramcontent.com/pod-product-compliance
Lightning Source LLC
Chambersburg PA
CBHW082104140626
46553CB00018B/635